Basic Primary Grammar provides the basics of grammar in a book that is easy-to-read and understand. Knowledge of grammar helps students improve their spoken and written language and become better communicators.

This book allows for the study of grammar at the sentence, clause and word level. With each new concept, exercises are included to allow students to practise and reinforce their knowledge.

Students are encouraged to analyse how texts are constructed and how language is used in a variety of situations. This provides a sound base for language development.

START HERE

3

Contents

unit topic   page

5

How to use this book...

This book is designed so that students can explore different aspects of grammar as the need arises. It is not meant to be worked through from beginning to end.

Contents

The contents page is an easy way to look for the area of grammar you wish to explore. For other grammar terms the glossary/index has a page reference and definition.

Sections

Each section covers a different area of grammar and can be studied as needed. Each section is divided into units. These units consist of a left hand information page and a right hand activity page.

Units

Each unit includes a clear definition of the grammatical term followed by examples. The student can then finish the exercises on the facing activity page.

Answers

Answers are supplied for all questions that have a specific response. Where answers may vary, none have been supplied.

Glossary and Index

These sections provide definitions for grammatical terms, and include page numbers where more information can be found. This is useful for cross-referencing any unfamiliar terms.

To use *Pascal's Basic Primary Grammar*

1. **Look in the contents or glossary/index.**
2. **Read the left hand page.**
3. **Answer the questions on the facing activity page.**
4. **Check your answers.**
5. **Revise any problem areas.**

no

&

8

ns

pronouns

9

Nouns

A noun is a <u>naming word</u>. It is the name of a person, animal, place, thing, or feeling.

Linda dog mountain hammer happiness

*The nouns are in **bold** in the following sentences:*

1. **Louise** collected the **parcel**.
2. My **dog Spot** sleeps in the **kennel**.
3. The **river** flowed quickly to the **sea**.
4. Her **happiness** was overwhelming.

*Nouns can be **singular**, one or **plural**, more than one — dog, dogs. Nouns have different ways of changing to the plural form.*

singular	plural
boy	boys
man	men
lady	ladies
tomato	tomatoes
knife	knives
sheep	sheep

Nouns can be divided into four groups

1. **Proper nouns** name a particular person or place and begin with a capital letter — Saturday, Jason, Australia

2. **Common nouns** are names common to all people or things of the same kind — woman, boy, month, suburb, tree, cat

3. **Collective nouns** name a collection of people or things — team, pack, group, crowd, navy (a collection of sailors)

4. **Abstract nouns** name feelings and ideas — pain, freedom, joy, sorrow

1. _Underline_ the nouns in this passage.

Mum and Dad, Clare and Hugh, went for a drive to Campbelltown, an outer suburb of Sydney. They were looking for a breeder who sold border collie pups. Clare and Hugh could hardly contain their excitement as the city gave way to larger blocks, more and more trees and the occasional farm.

2. _Make each of these nouns plural._

NOUNS	
Singular	**Plural**
baby	
mouse	
wolf	
half	
knife	
loaf	

3. _Jobs that people do are nouns. Write the names of six jobs that you know._

_____

_____

4. _Underline_ the proper nouns.

Jay, Simba, telephone, February, choir, Zimbabwe

5. _Underline_ the collective nouns.

eagle, flight, herd, ambulance, team, Sharon, army

6. _Underline_ the common nouns.

elephant, Diane, bottle, Anzacs, glue, dog, cloud, pencil

7. _Draw a line from the common nouns to their matching collective nouns._

lions	wood	mob	school
flowers	fish	army	bunch
soldiers	sheep	pride	stack

Noun Groups

A group of words <u>including a noun</u> that describes a person, place or thing.
A noun group can include adjectives, clauses or a number of linked nouns.

To find a noun group in a sentence ask the questions — Who is involved? What things, ideas or events are involved?

Who was in the castle?
The jolly, green giant was in the castle.
Who was ill?
All the animals in the circus were ill.
What has been painted?
The house across the road has been painted.
What is brand new?
The car that I have is brand new.

Creating descriptive noun groups is an important part of good writing.

In **narratives** noun groups describe the characters and the setting to make them specific to the story.

The **tired, listless boy** looked down at his **crumpled, dirty shirt** and groaned. How could he go and see the **School Principal Mr Henkle** looking like this? Peter thought of Mr Henkle sitting in his **spotlessly clean and organised office**. He was probably sitting there right now thinking up **Peter's ultimate punishment**.

In **factual writing** — reports, recounts, procedures, explanations, expositions and arguments — noun groups are also used to create strong images.

The **small, green tree frog**, living in **Queensland's ever-diminishing rainforests**, is under **the threat of extinction**.

12

ACTIVITY PAGE

1. _Underline_ the noun groups in the sentences.

a The crates of animals were loaded aboard.
b The skiff with the torn sail limped into the harbour.
c Many of the books which I owned have been given away.
d Some very rich desserts were served.
e The bird in the huge nest was an eagle.

2. Add _noun groups_ to these sentences.

a _____ were waiting at the gate.

b _____ appeared from over the hill.

c _____ were seen by the children.

d _____ was terrifying.

3. Use these _noun groups_ in sentences.

a the boys in red shirts

_____

b several athletic dancers

_____

c a large, overhanging branch

_____

4. Write _a short description of a dog you have known._

_____

_____

   Underline all the noun groups in your description.

5. Add _the words in the brackets to these sentences._

a The dog leapt at me.

_____ (large, hairy)

_____ (with big teeth)

b There's a monster.

_____ (huge, green, slobbering)

_____ (running after me)

Pronouns

A pronoun is a word that is used instead of a noun.

Instead of _Jack took Jack's book when Jack went to Jack's study_, we write _Jack took his book when he went to his study_.

The pronouns **his** and **he** are used to replace the noun **Jack**.

There are several groups of personal pronouns.

When we are speaking about ourselves
- **I** went to the show early.
- Come with **me**.
- **We** are playing tennis.
- Jack saw **us**.

When we are speaking to others
- **You** should clean the car.
- Go by **yourself**.

Pronouns for asking questions
- **Who** is there?
- **What** is the problem?
- **Whose** book is that?

PERSONAL PRONOUNS

Singular	Plural	Singular	Plural
I	we	she	they
me	us	her	theirs
mine	ours	he	yours
you	you	him	they
yours	ours	hers	whose
it	who		

14

1. <u>Underline</u> the pronouns in these sentences.

a He went with his brother.

b Did you go by yourself to their home?

c When I see your friends I will tell them you are here.

d 'Who is there?' she asked.

2. Rewrite these passages using pronouns.

a James opened James' book and got James' pencil and started James' homework.

_____

_____

b We saw the boys when the boys' sister told us where the boys were playing.

_____

_____

3. Write the correct pronouns in the passage below.

Jenny didn't know what hit _____. _____ looked down and there at _____ feet was a football. There was a group of boys playing on the oval. _____ must belong to _____.

Jenny was rubbing _____ head. When _____ looked over all of the boys were looking at _____. _____ were looking guilty. One of them called to _____.

"Sorry, but can _____ throw the ball?"

4. Make these sentences refer to more than one person by changing the pronouns.

a She hurt herself._____

b I have my books with me ._____

c He helped himself. _____

Problem pronouns

Sometimes it is difficult to decide whether to use I or me in a sentence.

Burt and **me** went to the shops.   Burt and **I** went to the shops.

In this case try splitting the sentence into two.

Burt went to the shops.

Me went to the shops.

I went to the shops.

So the correct usage is — **Burt and I went to the shops.**

Mum gave the cake to Kim and **me**.   Mum gave the cake to Kim and **I**.

Split the sentence again.

Mum gave the cake to Kim.

Mum gave the cake to me.

Mum gave the cake to I.

So the correct usage is — **Mum gave the cake to Kim and me.**

When to use **who** or **which**.

Who always refers to people.

There are many people outside **who** think we should stop.

Which refers to animals or things.

The giraffes in the zoo **which** escaped yesterday.

REMEMBER
The pronoun **you** stays the same for singular and plural use.
I love you all.

ACTIVITY PAGE

1. *Write the correct pronouns in these sentences.*

a Lee and _____ went for a ride on _____ bikes.

b You wouldn't believe what Maureen and _____ saw.

c Now there is a girl _____ knows her thoughts.

d The table _____ we shared.

e Jane and _____ went for a swim.

f The angry people _____ live down the street.

2. *Write the pronouns in these sentences.*

a There was nothing Mario or _____ could do.

b _____ want to be a fighter pilot.

c The dog _____ lost its collar.

d It must have been the boy behind you _____ did it.

e Zack and _____ are going to the beach.

f The cat sat next to _____ .

g The carpenter _____ did the job.

h The playground, _____ had just been cleaned,
was dirty again.

3. *Correct these sentences.*

a Don't leave the room unless I tell youse.

_____

b 'Why was youse here?' she asked.

_____

c Those hat is mine.

_____

Prepositions

The cat is **on** the bed.
The ball is **under** the bed.
Jana is **in** the bed.

The prepositions **on, under** and **in** all refer to the bed and show the relationship between the cat, the ball and Jana to the bed.

Some common prepositions include: in, on, up, under, over, across, behind, past, down, near, into, at, on top, next to, of, in between

Prepositional phrases begin with a preposition. Remember that phrases do not contain a verb.

They travelled **towards the city**.

The woman **in the red hat** is over there.

Some prepositions can also be adverbs. Remember that prepositions are always followed by a noun or pronoun and relate one thing to another.

I was **behind**. .... adverb
I was **behind the trees**. .... preposition

They walked **around**. .... adverb
They walked **around** the block. .... preposition

1. <u>Underline</u> the prepositions in these sentences.

a Jason walked past the school.

b Natassia is in the classroom.

c I put my shoes on top of the cupboard.

d Alex stood near the motorbike.

2. Use the picture to answer true or false to the following.

a The little girl is next to the big dog. _____

b The cat is on the woman's head. _____

c The boy is sitting on the rabbit hutch. _____

d The large man is next to the bird. _____

e The rabbit is in the cage. _____

f The man with the bird is in front of the rabbit hutch. _____

g The little girl is sitting on the dog. _____

h The large man is between the rabbit and the cat. _____

i The cat is behind the woman. _____

3. <u>Underline</u> the prepositional phrases in these sentences.

a On the trip over the desert the travellers moved through difficult terrain.

b They followed the path over the hill to the blue lake near the homestead.

c I ran down the road and Julie followed on her bike.

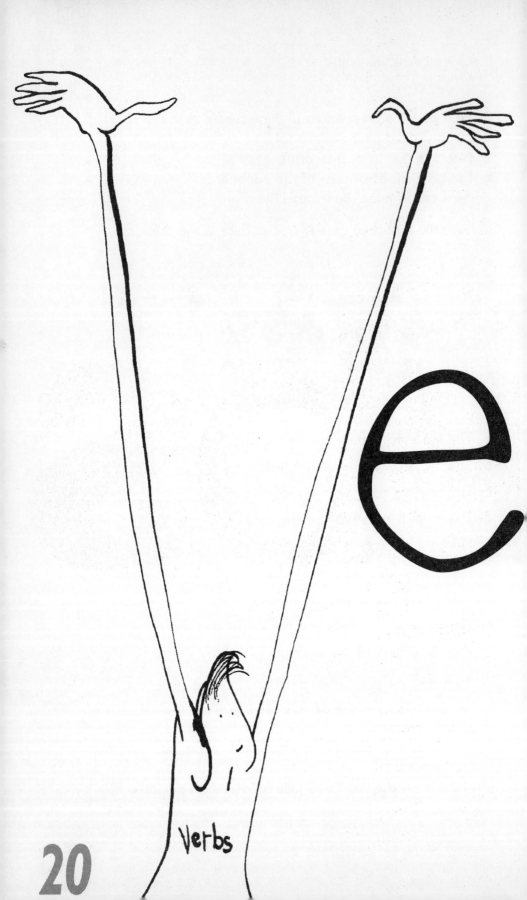

Verbs

20

rbs

Verbs

Verbs include doing, thinking, and saying words as well as states of being and having. Verbs are an essential part of a clause.

They **ran** up the hill.	doing or action verb
Aidan **rode** the horse.	
He **was worried** about the test.	thinking verb
Emily **knows** the way to the showground.	
She **spoke** softly to her cat.	saying verb
All the boys **had been told** what to do.	
The fireman **is** in the house.	being or having verb
Aisha **has had** a bad fever.	

Verbs have tense. This means they show whether the action is taking place in the present, in the past or in the future.

Present tense   I am **polishing** the table.

Past tense   I **polished** the table.

Future tense   I **will polish** the table.

Another **tense** *often used is* **timeless present** *and refers to actions that continue over time.*

Fish **swim** in the ocean.
Tigers **are** good hunters.
Children **enjoy** playing games.

All the verbs on this page are **finite verbs**. Finite verbs have a subject.
In the three sentences above the subjects are **fish**, **tigers** and **children**.

1. *Complete the table.*

base verb	past	present	future
ring			
leave			
bring			
fence			
drop			
tell			

2. *Write the correct form of the verb* **see** *in the following sentences.*
Choose from — see, sees, seen, seeing, saw

a I have _____ him there several times.

b Many of them were _____ the show.

c All of the students _____ the play.

3. *Write the correct form of the verb* **do** *in the following sentences.*
Choose from — do, does, done, doing, did

a Has Sharon _____ the work yet?

b Ian can _____ the shopping.

c The class were _____ their assignments?

d _____ Matthew live nearby?

4. *Change the verbs in these sentences to future tense.*

a The boy saw the horse.

_____

b The girls played in the sand.

_____

5. *Identify the verbs as action, thinking, saying or having-being verbs.*

a The boy has had a bad cold. _____

b The girl believed the story. _____

c Emily drove the car to the lake. _____

Types of **Verbs**

action verbs — He **ran** down the hill. Penny **climbed** the ladder.

thinking verbs — I **understand**. Carol **believed** him.

saying verbs — I **said** yes. She **yelled** at me. Chris **suggested** another way.

having or being verbs — Matt **has** the answer. Nick **was** here but Ned **is** here now.

The verbs above stand alone. They are the main verbs. There are many verbs that are made up of a main verb and one or more helping verbs. These helping verbs are called auxiliary verbs.

Sue **is painting** the house.
They **will be leaving** for America tomorrow.
He **should be coming** soon.

Verb groups with one or more auxiliary verbs are called compound verbs.

Voice: verbs can be active or passive.

Active voice
Charles **collected** the parcel.
Here Charles (the subject) does the action. **Collected** is the active form of the verb.
The active voice focuses on the person or thing doing the action.

Passive voice
The parcel **was collected** by Charles.
Here the parcel is having the action done to it. **Was collected** is the passive form of the verb.
The passive voice focuses on the person or thing affected by the action.

24

ACTIVITY PAGE

1. *Add verbs to this passage. Read the whole passage through to make sure it makes sense.*

Judith _____ down the hall. I'm late she _____.

She was very _____. This _____ the day of the final.

Her team _____ well all season and were the favourites.

2. <u>Underline</u> *the auxiliary (helping) verbs in these sentences.*

a They will be leaving at three o'clock.
b The grey horse has been jumping well.
c Have any of the children been seen at the cafe?
d The mouse is helping the lion.

3. *Use these compound verbs in sentences.*

a will be leaving

_____

b has been diving

_____

4. *Write five words you could use instead of 'said', in the following sentence: Sani said, "will you help me?".*

_____

_____

5. <u>Underline</u> *the verbs in these sentences and state whether they are in the active or passive voice.*

a Joe finished the work early. _____

b The truck was driven by my sister. _____

c Most of the students played netball. _____

6. *Change these sentences so that the verb is in the opposite voice.*

a Christina discovered the hole in the fence.

_____

b The painting was completed by the art student.

_____

Infinitives

The infinitive is the <u>name of the verb</u> eg. win, visit, ride. They usually begin with the word to and are not the main verbs in a sentence.

They came to visit their friend.
To find the lost treasure was going to be difficult.
She ran quickly to win the race.

The infinitive often does the work of other parts of speech.

The horse to ride is in the paddock.
'to ride' describes the horse. Describing words are adjectives
To visit his neighbours he rode his new bike.
'to visit' tells why he rode. Words which tell why, how, when and where are adverbs.

Participles

Another type of verb is the participle. There are **past** participles and **present** participles.

Regular verbs are those verbs which use **ed, d, en, n** or **t** to form the past participle and **ing** to form the present participle. Past participles usually follow **has, have, had** or **was**.

verb	past participle	present participle
jump	(have) jumped	(am) jumping
cry	(had) cried	(is) crying

Irregular verbs are those which form the past participle in a different way.

verb	past participle	present participle
ring	(have) rung	(am) ringing
buy	(have) bought	(am) buying

1. *Choose the correct present participle to complete these sentences.*
   mending running fishing buying crying

a The girl _____ the fence is my sister.

b I was _____ for the bus when I fell over.

c The children are _____ from the pier.

d She sat down and started _____.

e I am _____ milk for my mother.

2. *Use each infinitive phrase in a sentence.*

a to follow the car

_____

b to see her friend

_____

c to fight the monster

_____

3. *Rewrite these sentences so the events are happening in the present.*

a She dived into the pool.

_____

b They drove past us.

_____

c I told him.

_____

d Josh travelled by bus to the game.

_____

e The police followed the car.

_____

4. *Write the base form of these verbs.*

a ridden _____   b meant _____

c chosen _____   d dealt _____

e understood _____   f met _____

Verb groups

A verb group is a group of words that describes the activities taking place and includes the main verb. Verb groups are sometimes known as processes.

Action (doing) verb groups	He **has been completing** the work. Susie **is going to repair** the net.
Thinking verb groups	Steve **did not completely understand** the problem. **I have never believed** that story.
Saying verb groups	Lorraine **did suggest** a good method. She **had been asking politely** for some time.
Having or being verb groups	Linda **was not being** very polite. She **has been sulking** all afternoon.

Verb groups are useful when studying a text as they describe what's going on.

Look at this passage. The verb groups are in the dark type.

They **decided to walk** to the restaurant. Jill was **going to have** lasagne. Aidan **didn't know what he wanted**. He **was going to look** at the menu. When they arrived their parents **told the waiter that they had booked** a table. The waiter **told us we would have to wait** as our table **wasn't ready** yet.

The passage above has a variety of verb groups. Verb groups give a detailed description of the activities taking place.

ACTIVITY PAGE

1. _Underline_ the verb groups in these sentences.

a The car has been regularly making a shuddering sound.
b The cows have been grazing quietly all morning.
c The boy had been known to tell lies.
d He wanted to complete the work.
e Have you been delivering the leaflets?
f Is the painter finished yet?

2. Identify the verb groups as action, thinking, saying, or having–being groups.

a The boy has had a bad cold._____

b The girl believed the story. _____

c Emily drove the car to the lake. _____

d Jason told Sharni the answer. _____

3. _Underline_ the verb groups in this passage.

Fotini started to feel hungry as she worked. There was quite a bit more to do before she could finish. She decided to keep working for another hour. After twenty minutes her stomach began to growl.
"Just a bit longer," she thought.

4. Write a short passage which recounts a recent experience that you've had. Express your actions, thoughts and feelings.

_____

_____

_____

_____

_____

_____

Underline all the verb groups in your passage.

Adjec
&
Ad

30

tives

verbs

Adjectives

> Adjectives are describing words that add meaning to a noun.

An adjective tells
- *what kind*
- *how many*
- *how much*
- *which person or thing.*

What kind of day is it?
It is a **cold** day.

How many children?
Several children played in the park.

Which cat?
That cat belongs to Linda.

There is often more than one adjective used to describe a noun or noun group.
Many frisky, young foals played in the paddock.
The farm had **rich, black, fertile** soil.

Describers, numeratives and determiners
Some adjectives are **describers**.

There were **beautiful** sunsets every night.
The farm had **fertile** soil.

The words **beautiful** and **fertile** describe the noun.

Some adjectives are **numerative**.
The word numerative means number.

Several children went to the park.
Ten cars were loaded onto the transporter.

The words **several** and **ten** tell how many.

Some adjectives are **determiners**.
They are used to specify which noun is being spoken of.

That cat belongs to Linda.
Those animals were taken away.

ACTIVITY PAGE

1. *Write suitable adjectives for these nouns.*

a _____ animal   b _____ bag

c _____ telephone   d _____ cards

e _____ monster   f _____ frog

2. *Use each group of adjectives in a sentence.*

a cool, clear sparkling

_____

b some sweet juicy

_____

c large, green, hairy

_____

3. *Add adjectives to these sentences.*

The _____ children went on a _____ trip.

They visited _____ island.

The _____ island was surrounded by _____ water.

In the _____ water were _____ fish.

The _____ fish ate _____ seaweed.

The _____ children had a _____ holiday.

4. *Add adjectives to these sentences. Then label them describer,*
numerative, or determiner.

a _____ stamps belong to Sharni.   _____

b _____ truck delivered the food.   _____

c Is _____ car wrecked?   _____

d _____ children attended the concert.   _____

e Carla collected _____ shells.   _____

f _____ lorikeets were in the aviary.   _____

33

Comparative Adjectives

Adjectives can be used to compare things.

It is a small dog.

This dog is smaller than the other.

This is the smallest dog.

When comparing two things use the comparative form.

When comparing more than two things use the superlative form.

base	comparative	superlative
big	bigger	biggest
strong	stronger	strongest
happy	happier	happiest

*Many adjectives simply add **er** for the comparative and **est** for the superlative form. Note that words ending in **y** drop the **y** and add **ier** or **iest**.*

In other cases we need to add more for the comparative and most for the superlative.

base	comparative	superlative
beautiful	more beautiful	most beautiful
careful	more careful	most careful

Some words are irregular and change altogether.

good/well	better	best
bad	worse	worst
little	less	least

REMEMBER
Do not use double comparatives or double superlatives.

The **more faster** boat won the race.

The word **more** makes the phrase **more faster boat** a double comparative.

The sentence should be — The faster boat won the race.

34

1. *Complete this table.*

base	comparative	superlative
small	_____	_____
lovely	_____	_____
good	_____	_____
interesting	_____	_____
clean	_____	_____
difficult	_____	_____
unhappy	_____	_____
simple	_____	_____

2. *Use the comparative and superlative forms of the adjective* **tall** *to fit these sentences.*

a This building is _____ than the other.

b This is the _____ tree in the district.

c My brother is _____ than you.

d Carol is the _____ girl in her class.

3. *Use the comparative and superlative form of the adjective* **grand** *to fit these sentences.*

a This palace is _____ than the other one.

b Of all the buildings this is by far the _____ of all.

4. *Use the comparative form of an adjective in these sentences.*

a Jill is _____ than Ben.

b The box is _____ than the chair.

c The dog ran _____ than me.

d The ice is _____ than my skin.

5. *Are these sentences correct? Cross out the incorrect word.*

a As the sun rose more higher the cows sought shade.

b It is the most loveliest dress she had ever bought.

c This will make you feel more better.

d It was the most wettest year on record.

Order of Adjectives

Adjectives can be divided into words that give opinions or words that describe.

Opinion adjectives	descriptive adjectives
nice, horrible, naughty	black, little, Chinese, soft
lovely, best, worst,	big, round, hard
comfortable, nasty	leather, ancient, modern

When using two or more adjectives opinion adjectives go before descriptive adjectives.

Isn't he a **nice, little** puppy.

That is a **lovely, new, blue** shirt.

Opinion adjectives often tell how a person (or people) feels about something.
A lot of these adjectives end in **ed** or **ing**.

The football game was **boring**.

It was a very **disappointing** day.

Her parents were **worried**.

The film was absolutely **terrifying**.

He was **pleased** with his test results.

There are six basic types of descriptive adjectives. You are unlikely to use all of them at once but it can be useful to think through different ideas when you are writing.

The six basic types of descriptive adjectives are:
size shape age colour nationality material
The above is also the normal order when using more than one adjective. For example, if using a size, shape and colour adjective you would normally write

A large, round, red basketball.

The small, rectangular, green box.

1. *Write adjectives to describe the following.*

      opinion   size   shape   age   colour

a A _____ couch.

b The_____ car.

c A _____ ball.

d The_____ dog.

e A _____ bag.

2. *Add **ed** or **ing** to the **bold** words to correct the sentences.*
When I got up this morning I was very **tir** _____ so I went
run _____. I soon remembered how **excit** _____ today was
going to be. I wasn't going to be **bor** _____ today. Our whole
class were going to see a really **interest** _____ film about
spiders. I was ready to be **scar** _____ and **thrill** _____ by it.

3. *Use the following in sentences.*

a large, new blue

_____

b round green

_____

c ugly, large leather

_____

d young Vietnamese

_____

e beautiful, small pink

_____

4. *Write an **opinion** adjective in the following.*

a I think football is _____.

b Barbie dolls are _____.

c My dog is _____.

d I _____ ice-cream.

Adverbs

An adverb tells **how**, **when**, **where** or **why** something happened. Adverbs add meaning to verbs, adjectives or other adverbs (not nouns).

How did the men walk?
The men walked **slowly**.

When will they arrive?
They will arrive **soon**.

Where did the pony stand?
The pony stood **there**.

how adverbs
badly, softly, beautifully, gently, easily, sometimes, well, quickly

when adverbs
during, yesterday, today, tomorrow, next year, last night, at night, in the morning

where adverbs
there, here, next to, near to, in, on, everywhere,

REMEMBER
Some adverbs are built from adjectives by adding 'ly'.

adjective	adverb
real	real**ly**
heavy	heavi**ly**
particular	particular**ly**

He plays **real** well.
The word **real** is an adjective but the adverb **really** is needed.

ACTIVITY PAGE

1. _Underline_ the adverbs in these sentences.

a She sang the song delightfully.
b Soon we shall arrive at the city.
c The animal chewed the meat greedily.
d For two hours the students waited there.
e The children completed the work eagerly.
f Sometimes James would go to the theatre.

2. Use these adverbs in suitable sentences.

a often

_____

c late

_____

d seldom

_____

3. Many adverbs are built from adjectives. Change the word
shown in **bold** type into an adverb.

a Sherry is a **neat** worker. She works _____.
b He acts in a **strange** way. He acts _____.
c They played **noisy** games. They played _____.

4. Write suitable adverbs for these sentences.

a The aircraft dropped (how) _____ to the ground.
b They had not seen the dog (where) _____.
c The guests will arrive (when) _____.

5. Correct these sentences.

a It rained real heavily this afternoon. _____
b It is a particular heavy box. _____
c This is the first real good book I've bought. _____

39

Types of Adverbs

**Adverbs are often used to make a verb
weaker or stronger.**

Time adverbs   **when** the action happened

Manner adverbs   **how** the action was done

Place adverbs   **where** the action occurred

We **really** laughed. — manner
Are you coming **tomorrow**. — time
They **nearly** ran into each other. — manner
The book is over **there**. — place
I **sometimes** go out at night. — time
Nobody came **near**. — place

Adverbs like adjectives have degree

He played **well**. — positive
He played **better** than his brother. — comparative
Peter played the **best** of all. — superlative

Tom saw it **clearly**. — positive
She saw it **more clearly** than her brother. comparative. — degree
I saw it the **most clearly** of all. — superlative degree

1. *Choose one of the adverbs to complete each sentence.*

sometimes, usually, always, occasionally, often, never, hardly ever

a I_____ help around the house.

b I_____ go to a restaurant for dinner.

c I_____ brush my teeth in the morning.

d I_____ wash the dishes.

e I_____ watch TV in the afternoon.

f I_____ eat spaghetti.

g I_____ use a computer.

2. *Add an adverb to these sentences.*

a The students left the school _____ (how).

b _____ (when)it rained _____ (how).

c Jane went to the show _____ (when).

d The principal said `Come here _____ (when).

e No one is to go _____ (where) the broken fence.

3. *In each pair of sentences the adverb is placed in a different position. Tick the correct one.*

a (i) I am really disappointed in you. _____
   (ii) I am disappointed really in you. _____

b (i) There was an accident almost. _____
   (ii) There was almost an accident. _____

c (i) He talked very quickly _____
   (ii) He very quickly talked. _____

d (i) The bucket was completely empty. _____
   (ii) The bucket was empty completely. _____

e (i) The cake was eaten partly. _____
   (ii) The cake was partly eaten. _____

f (i) It was very interesting. _____
   (ii) It was interesting very. _____

g (i) The party was absolutely wonderful. _____
   (ii) The party was wonderful absolutely. _____

Sent

Cla

ences and uses

Simple Sentences

Simple sentences have <u>one clause</u> and make sense on their own. They always contain a verb and often include a noun.

A sentence begins with a capital letter and ends with a full stop, question mark or exclamation mark.

Linda watched the show.
Where are you going?
Yes, I've done it!

There are four types of sentences.

STATEMENTS

The girl was watching the horses.
She collected the parcels.
My brother is eight years old.

QUESTIONS

Are you going to the movies?
Can the work be done?
When will the cake be cooked?

COMMANDS OR REQUESTS

These are sometimes called directives because they can give directions, provide advice or warnings, or invite.

Sit down. (command)
Pass the salt please. (request)
Maybe you should rest for awhile. (advice)
Look out for that truck. (warning)
Come to the show with me. (invitation)

EXCLAMATIONS

Exclamations are abrupt or excited comments.

Ouch, that hurts!   What a hot day!   She's done it!

1. *Label these sentences: statement, question, command, request or exclamation.*

a Where has Billy gone?
b Turn the light off in there.
c Trini has left for the city.
d Look out!
e Why don't you look under the bed?
f Please help your sister with the dishes.

2. *Are these groups of words sentences? Write yes or no.*

a All of us.
b Many friends.
c Please take the parcel.
d By the river.
e Have you seen Aisha?
f To the coast.
g Can it be done?

Make any word groups from question 2 into complete sentences.

_____

_____

_____

_____

_____

3. *Underline the verbs in these sentences.*

a My brother found the missing money.
b All the people went to the fair.
c Where did Hank go last week?
d Sven gave the present to Julie.
e They told me the news.
f Ned collected the mail from the box.

Clauses

The group of words involved with the verb make up the clause. A clause contains a verb and its subject.

I waited for him. (simple sentence — one clause)
Clauses can be divided into two types: independent and dependent.
Independent clauses can stand on their own.
I wanted to go to the fair.
Dependent clauses do not make complete sense on their own. Dependent clauses need an independent clause to make a sentence.
This is the car that I own.
'This is the car' is the independent clause
'that I own' is the dependent clause.

Complex sentences

A complex sentence has an independent clause and one or more dependent clauses.

I wanted to go to the fair   which was at the showground.
independent   **dependent**

In this next case the dependent clause is **embedded**.
The boat, which carried three people, **sailed out of the harbour**.

The boat sailed out of the harbour — **independent**
which carried three people — **dependent**.

Compound sentences

Compound sentences have two or more independent clauses.

Jenny didn't collect the mail and she forgot her pencils.
I can jump high and Penny can run fast.
The two independent clauses are connected by **and**.

ACTIVITY PAGE

unit 16

1. Which of these are complex sentences?

a I found the lost dog.
b Where is the cat that was injured?
c She did not collect the parcel in the morning.
d Many of those who were ill could not continue.

2. Combine these pairs of sentences into a complex sentence.

a Here are the cattle. They ate the crops.

_____

b Romana owns the car. It is by the garage.

_____

3. Write the two simple sentences that form these complex sentences.

a The students who came here did not complete the work.

_____

_____

b I enjoyed the show which was full of action.

_____

_____

4. Are any of these sentences compound sentences?

a All of them visited the park and the picnic grounds.
b They came and watched the game.
c He completed the job but was very tired.
d My cousin went to the dance but she did not stay late.

5. Combine each pair of sentences into compound sentences.

a Dario went to the field. He climbed the mountain.

_____

b Sally plays the piano. She cannot play the flute.

_____

c My brother goes to the class. He might see the film.

_____

M**oo**d

Language is used to ask questions, inform, make inquiries, suggestions and commands. The mood of a clause, sentence or conversation depends on the usage. There are three moods — **declarative**, **imperative** and **interrogative**.

Declarative mood	Charles found the treasure. subject verb	**statement**
Imperative mood	Find the treasure! verb subject	**command**
Interrogative mood	Where is Charles?	**question**

In different situations statements, commands and questions are made with differing degrees of certainty.

STATEMENT	He definitely found it. I think he found it. He may have found it. I'm not sure whether he knows where it is.
COMMAND	Find it! Would you find it, please. Please look for it. Maybe you'll find it if you look. If you could find it, I would appreciate it.
QUESTION	Where is it? Have you found it? Can you find it? Could you look for it soon?

Degree of certainty

High degree words include: certainly, definitely, must, will, always, can, has to

Low degree words include: maybe, could, sometimes, possibly, might, probably, may

1. *Rewrite the following with a high degree of certainty.*

a I don't think I can go.

_____

b Do you think you can do it?

_____

c Maybe the boxes are over there.

_____

d I think I saw him.

_____

e Can you get up soon?

_____

f Jill may come to the party.

_____

g Ellen sometimes plays tennis on a Friday.

_____

2. *List four things you have to do at school. Write each one as
a sentence.*

_____

_____

_____

_____

3. *Write four different ways that you could ask someone to come
to a party.*

_____

_____

_____

_____

Questions

Questions are asked to obtain more information.
There are two main types of questions.

1. Closed questions

These questions require a simple 'yes/no' or short answer.

Is Ursula here?
Do you like chocolate?
Has Nick been here?
How does Jake take his tea?
When did they arrive?
Where did you put it?

2. Open questions

These require a longer response.

How would you solve this problem?
What do you think about feral cats?
How do you feel about Greenpeace?
What can be done about toxic waste?

Creating questions

When creating questions for a specific purpose — interviewing someone about his/her life, finding out the rules of a game — it is important to ask useful questions. Think about what you want to know and create questions accordingly.

1. *Use these words to finish the questions.*

who   what   when   where   which   whose   why   how

a _____ do you live?

b _____ do you have for lunch?

c _____ are your friends?

d _____ do you get home?

e _____ is in the box?

f _____ is that boy over there?

2. *Create a **closed** question or an **open** question for each of the following.*

a Finding the nearest toilet.

_____

_____

b Asking a friend to help you.

_____

_____

c Asking someone about his/her swimming ability.

_____

_____

3. *Write some interview questions for a favourite book or television character?*
Character's name: _____

_____

_____

_____

Sentence parts

Verb
All sentences contain at least one verb.

Subject
The subject is the person or thing doing the action.

Jessica played in the park.   Who played? Jessica.
Is the car parked behind the shed?   What is parked? The car.

The subject is often left out in commands or requests.
Don't do that   (You is left out.)
Collect the parcel.   (You is left out.)

Object
In a sentence the action is affecting the object.
Maria will collect the **parcel**.
The parcel is the object.

The parcel is the direct object. It is directly affected by the verb.
In some sentences there is more than one object.

She gave Jack the book.
The **verb** is gave.
The **subject** is she.
The **direct object** is book and the **indirect object** is Jack.

REMEMBER
A singular subject takes a singular verb.
The boy **is** working in the shop.

A plural subject takes a plural verb.
The boys **are** working in the shop.

1. _Underline_ the verbs in these sentences.

a How happy the little girl is.
b The newspaper was delivered to the door.
c Can you do it?

2. _Underline_ the subjects in these sentences.

a Where did she go last week?
b They all went to Bondi beach.
c At dusk, all the lights came on.

3. _Underline_ the direct objects in these sentences.

a Have you signed the letter yet?
b Take this out as quickly as you can.
c Justine moved the chairs into the hall.

4. Are there **indirect** objects in these sentences? If so, _underline_ them.

a Sven gave the present to her.
b Yiu passed Linda the parcel.
c They told me the news.

5. Write the **verb, subject, object** order of these sentences.
The first one has been done for you.

a I like icecream. **subject verb object**
b Jim plays football. _____
c Alex was talking to Carol. _____
d The book that I gave you is mine. _____

6. Are these sentences correct? Write the correct word on the line.

a Several boys is collecting the mail. _____
b Goats, sheep and donkeys was grazing in the field. _____
c Emily, Aisha and Marlo is waiting at the gate. _____
d Hundreds of cars was held up at the bridge. _____

Sentences & Meaning

Another way of describing a sentence is to discuss how the words are used to provide meaning.

Noun groups (participants)
— the people, things, ideas and events involved.

Verb groups (processes)
— the actions or activities taking place.

Adverbs and prepositional phrases
(circumstances)
— how, when, where or why the actions take place.

Who?	**Action?**	**Where?**
My young brother	was running	in the race.
(noun group)	(verb group)	(prepositional phrase)
participant	process	circumstance

What?	**Action?**	**Where?**
The large black cat	is sitting very comfortably	on the armchair.
(noun group)	(verb group)	(adverb group)
participant	process	circumstance

Action?	**What?**	**Where?**
There was	a loving atmosphere	at the christening.
(verb group)	(noun group)	(prepositional phrase)
process	participant	circumstance

1. _Underline_ the participants (noun groups) in these sentences.

a All of the children went to the city.
b I will go.
c Care and attention to detail are required.
d A box with a green lid was found.

2. _Underline_ the circumstances (adverbs and prepositional phrases) in the following.

a I want to go to the beach on the weekend.
b The classroom was very noisy.
c Look at the way those cats play with each other.
d The boxes were overflowing with old toys.

3. Label each part of the following sentences.

a At the yearly show   _____
   the riders from out west   _____
   competed   _____
   for the many trophies   _____
   on display.   _____

b The scholars   _____
   read   _____
   the ancient documents.   _____

c The tribes   _____
   lived peacefully   _____
   in the valley.   _____

d At the time   _____
   the young boy   _____
   wasn't interested   _____
   in reading or writing.   _____

kiNg
1se

Articles

You use **a** and **an** with singular nouns.
The can be used in front of all nouns.

When something is first talked of, **a** or **an** are used. **The** is used when referring back to something.

I saw **an** ice-cream that I'd like. **The** ice-cream is vanilla with chocolate coating.

a & an

You use **a** and **an** with singular nouns.
There is **a** horse.
I'd like **an** orange.
You use **a** when the following word starts with a consonant sound.
I just saw a unicorn. (initial sound — **y**)
They have a car.
You use **an** when the following word starts with a vowel sound.
He was an honourable man. (initial sound — **o**)
He has an egg.

The

The can be used in front of all nouns, singular or plural. It is used when referring back to something. **The** is known as the definite article.
I bought a sandwich and then I dropped **the** sandwich.
I bought some sandwiches and then I dropped **the** sandwiches.

58

ACTIVITY PAGE

1. *Place **a** or **an** in the following sentences.*

a I'd like _____ sandwich, _____ orange juice

  and _____ packet of sultanas, please.

b Alfred owns _____ dog, _____ cat

  and _____ owl.

c He is _____ unique person.

d Is that _____ university or _____ college.

e It is _____ honour to serve you.

2. *Write **a, an** or **the** in the following.*

a Alisha went for _____walk up _____ mighty

  mountain. _____ mountain was very tall.

  She had on _____ new pair of walking shoes and

  _____ enormous hat. Before long _____

  shoes began to rub and _____ hat got heavier

  and heavier.

3. *Write the correct word in the following.*

a I went to _____ party. _____ party was

  very good.

b Pass me _____ apple, please. Yes, _____ red

  one will do.

c I'd like _____ ham sandwich, please. Can I have

  mustard on _____ sandwich too.

d Helen has _____ small toy car. _____ toy car

  was broken yesterday.

Connecting Words

Maria went to the shop.
Ned went to the shop.
Maria **and** Ned went to the shop.

The most common connecting words are:

and but or so yet because as both if before since like for

Connecting words are important as they make writing flow smoothly. Connecting words are also known as **conjunctions**.

Compare these two passages:

James was going out. It was cold. He put on a jumper. He put a jacket on as well. He stepped outside. A blast of cold wind blew in his face.

James was going out **but** it was cold. He put **both** his jumper **and** his jacket on. **As** he stepped outside, a blast of cold wind blew in his face.

Connecting words join words, phrases and clauses.

Joining single words: Sad **but** true.

Joining phrases: The beach was very crowded **like** last year.

Joining clauses
He was angry **yet** Jenny was calm.

More connecting words

however therefore until though where although wherever whenever since while once neither nor if

1. <u>Underline</u> the connecting words in these sentences.

a Slowly but eagerly they opened the chest.
b Neither Freya nor Ned did the work.
c Near the fence and beside the creek the children played.
d The fencing was done neatly and quickly.
e Many of them noticed the birds in the trees or in the shrubs.

2. Use connecting words and join the following.

a two adjectives _____
b two nouns _____
c two adverbs _____

3. Combine these pairs of sentences using connecting words.

a There are the parrots. There are the galahs.

_____

b Fotini owns the car. The car isn't working.

_____

c The boys went into town. The boys saw a movie.

_____

4. Place connecting words in these sentences.

a He went home _____ a bath.
b Christina touched it to see _____ it was not _____ cold.
c Joanne _____ Chris arrived to take down the sign.
d He was here _____ three o'clock.

5. Place connecting words in the following passage.

In the morning everyone _____ Billy got up. Billy stayed in
bed _____ slept. Billy had not been well _____ three
days. Aisha had a shower _____ got dressed.
She did it quietly _____ as not to wake Billy.
Aisha couldn't wait _____ he was better _____ she
missed having him to talk to.

Misused Words

This unit covers commonly misused words.

Double negatives

Don't put two negatives together. It doesn't make sense.

I'm not saying nothing. ✗   You should say, "I'm not saying anything."

I don't want none. ✗   You should say, "I don't want any."

Seen/saw

I saw you last night. ✔   I seen you last night. ✗

If you get confused about **seen** and saw just remember:

saw can be used on its own — I saw him.

seen needs a helping verb — I have seen him.

Did/done

I did it. ✔   I done it. ✗

did can be used on its own — She did it.

done needs a helping word — She has done it. (She's done it)

Two, to, too

Two is the number 2.

To can be used in many ways: from here to there, to do something, to push, to and fro.

Too is always an adverb: She is too much. He is clever too.

Should have/should've

When speaking **should've** can sound like **should of**. "Should of" is never right.

ACTIVITY PAGE

1. *Correct the following.*

a I don't know nothing.

_____

b No one don't care about me

_____

c I never go nowhere

_____

2.

a I just seen him downstairs

_____

3.

a I already done it.

_____

b The girls have did it already.

_____

4.

a. I was going too go but it cost two much.

_____

b. There are to many feral cats.

_____

c The girls were pushed too and fro.

_____

5.

a That box should of been picked up hours ago.

_____

b I should of known he would be late.

_____

Writing tips

Good writing is clear and easy to understand. This involves considering who the reader will be and what you are trying to tell them.

Before you start writing, make a plan.
Begin by thinking about the whole piece. Who is the audience and what are you trying to tell them?

1. **List the points that you could include**.

2. **Work on the sequence of events or ideas**.
   Number your points from one onwards. This may be fairly simple for an information report but a story may be told in many different ways. It can be written in chronological order or you could start at the main event and work backwards explaining why it happened.

3. **Now think of the paragraphs**.
   A paragraph is a group of sentences on the same subject or idea. A new paragraph starts on a new line and is used to introduce: a person, a place, a different time or a new idea.

4. **Be particular about your first and last paragraph**.
   Does the first paragraph grab the reader's attention and tell something about the whole piece? Does the last paragraph sum up the piece? Remember this is read last and can leave a lasting impression.

5. **Read through what you have written**.
   Does it tell the reader everything he or she needs to know? Are any sentences or paragraphs too long? Does your piece flow well? Is it interesting?

6. When you are happy with the content, double-check for any spelling or punctuation errors.

1. *Make a list of the points you would include if writing on one of the following topics.*

What I did yesterday The monster in my garden A report on spiders

_____

_____

_____

_____

_____

_____

_____

_____

2. *Give each of your points a number to help you put them in order.*

3. *Now write your opening paragraph.*

_____

_____

_____

_____

_____

_____

_____

_____

Punctuation

Capital letters

Capital letters are used for:
The first letter in a sentence.
The first letter in names — books, plays, poems, people, places,
pets, days, months, countries, states, towns, streets, mountains,
rivers, oceans, films, songs.
For I (personal pronoun).
Titles, initials.
The first letter in a new line of poetry.

Mick and Sam went to Allenstown.
Have you read the book 'Kidnapped'?
His cat Simba is an Abyssinian cat.

He worked until Friday the 1st of August.
I saw Captain Hurley.
Mr Len Bevan BA opened the building.

Full stops

Full stops show the end of a statement or command sentence.

Abbreviations

They also show abbreviations.

adj. for adjective max. for maximum

There are **no** full stops when the first letter of each word is used.

ACT   Australian Capital Territory
OECD   Organisation for Economic Cooperation and Development

Acronyms

ANZAC   Australian and New Zealand Army Corps
LOTE   Languages other than English

There are **no** full stops for abbreviations which use the first and last letter of
the word.

Mgr — Manager   Mr — Mister
Col — Colonel   Lt — Lieutenant

There are **no** full stops for units of measure.

cm — centimetre   ha — hectare
kg — kilogram   L — litre

ACTIVITY PAGE

1. *Underline the letters that need to be capitals.*

a jack and i read the book *jungle patrol* last july.
b in the poem 'hard labour' norfolk island is mentioned.
c on wednesday phil and romana went by train to bathurst to visit 'ellendale stud'.
d mrs j c curry visited the coffs harbour public school.
e in february i took my dog to anson island.
f in the novel *australian outback* the town of alice springs is featured.

2. *Write abbreviations for the following.*

a Technical and Further Education _____
b Litres _____
c Cubic centimetres _____
d Missus _____
e Street _____
f Queensland and Northern Territory Air Services _____
g Australian Capital Territory _____
h Wednesday _____
i Compact disc _____
j Video cassette recorder _____
k Captain _____
l Northern Territory _____
m Doctor _____

3. *Add full stops where needed and begin each new sentence with a capital letter. Use a red pen.*

He knew it would be hard but this was impossible the finish line was a blur in the distance he had to keep running his lungs hurt and his throat burned he needed to stop, but he couldn't this race was so important to him

Punctuation

Question marks

Question marks are needed at the end of any sentence that is a question.

Do you know how to make bread?

'Where is the car?' asked Steven.

Sometimes a question is asked in an **indirect way** and does not require a question mark.

I asked him what he said. — **indirect**.

What did he say? — **direct**.

Exclamation marks

Exclamation marks end sentences where strong emotions or reactions are expressed. Many exclamation sentences are quite short.

Ouch! I've cut my hand.

Good try!

How could you do that!

Colon

The colon is used to introduce lists. The lists may be: words, phrases, clauses or quotations.

She bought lots of fruit including: apples, bananas, pineapples, oranges, peaches and plums.

The groups played in several areas: behind the shed, near the wagon wheel, beside the old bridge and in the hayloft.

Semicolon

The semicolon can be used to join two short linked sentences and to separate complex lists.

I like chocolate; Alfred prefers ice-cream.

The furniture removed was an antique mahogany table with carved legs; a ten-drawer dresser with pearl inlay; a three metre long antique sideboard with mirror; and a new piano stool.

1. *Add full stops, question marks or exclamation marks where needed in these sentences.*

a Help They are getting away

b 'Why are you here   asked Tom

c 'Quick, get out of here   shouted Joan

d 'What is the capital of Tasmania   enquired Tim

e 'What a great save   said the reporter excitedly

f 'How do you reach Lake Placid ' asked Lee

g I asked him what he saw

h "What a surprise Who organised this " asked Mum

2. *Write a list of questions that you would ask your favourite rock star.*

_____

_____

_____

_____

_____

_____

3. *Place colons in the following sentences.*

a There were many birds in the cage finches, sparrows, lovebirds, pigeons and galahs.

b Carrie had driven several cars a Ferrari, a Porsche, a BMW, an Audi and a Bentley.

c There were books on many subjects in the pile maths, English, social studies and computers.

4. *Write a sentence using a semicolon.*

_____

_____

_____

Punctuation

Commas

Commas are used to show short pauses in writing. They are used in various ways.

Separating nouns

At the show they saw Porsches, Ferraris, BMW's, Audis, Bentleys and Cobras.

Separating adjectives and adverbs

Caroline was a tall, bright, talented, industrious girl.
The announcer spoke loudly, clearly and intelligently during the contest.

After introductory words

In fact, he had no way of knowing the answer.
Look, it is not very clear to me.
In addition, she won the two hundred metre race.

Separating different parts of speech

His younger sister, Emily, had completed Year 7.
Sharni, leave that alone.
I went to meet Brian, the new boy, by the shed.

Separating parts of long sentences

At the beach we played on the sand for some time, and at the river we went para-sailing.

1. *Put commas in the following sentences.*

a Many of the young frisky ponies galloped across the paddock.

b Pelicans ducks and swans were on the lake.

c The cold damp room was very gloomy.

d Nancy Annie Loma and May went to Cairns.

e A wise old brown owl was sitting in the tree.

f Strange ghostly mysterious shapes were seen.

g Speedboats cruisers kayaks and yachts were out on the river.

h Ponies quarter-horses appaloosas and Australian stock horses were at the show.

i Of course the rider came to no harm.

j Last year the students played football on the newly built oval and enjoyed swimming in the new Olympic pool.

k My big brother Mat lives in Singapore.

l 'Excuse me can you tell me where the shopping centre is?'

m Did you know that Ms Jenkins the Year 4 teacher is away today.

2. *Rewrite the following sentences adding capitals, full stops and commas.*

a i'm afraid of the dark

_____

b i don't like bugs mice and rats

_____

c the duck was small wet cold and hungry

_____

d there i was alone scared and hungry

_____

e she saw a beautiful craggy old tree

_____

f mr hines the principal said we could go

_____

_____

Punctuation

 Quotation marks (inverted commas)
Quotation marks are used to:
* *show the exact words of a speaker*
* *enclose the names of books and stories*
* *quote words and phrases from text*

Exact words of a speaker

Zsuzsi said,"I don't like that house".
"Where are you going?" asked George.
"All of the students are in the hall", the teacher answered.
"That boy", said Mr Pike,"is not paying attention."

Notice the two sets of quotation marks and the placement of commas.

Enclosing special names

I enjoyed the book "Struggle to the Sun".
The poem "Ode to Autumn" is difficult to understand.
The ship, "Rainbow Warrior", sailed into the Pacific.

Quotations within quotations use the single form.

"The choir sang 'Advance Australia Fair' very well", said the judge.

Now read this conversation.

"Quickly close the door!" whispered Jane.
"Why?" asked Mary curiously.
"Well, I just heard someone outside", replied Jane anxiously.
"Oh! You are imagining things again", said Mary confidently.

When there is more than one speaker a new line begins when another person starts to speak.

Notice the placement of exclamation and question marks, commas and full stops.

1. *Add quotation marks to these sentences.*

a He is going to the show   said Rhonda.

b Mark saw the young filly   cried Bill.

c Take it out at once   said Dad.

d I'm sure I know the answer   replied Andrew.

e Look out for the falling brick   shouted Amanda.

2. *Add quotation marks to these broken quotations.*

a The girl   he replied   can hardly lift it.

b Well   the stranger asked   where is the gift?

c If you travel south   he explained   you will reach the forest.

d This view   announced the driver   is the most famous in
the district.

e Oh dear   groaned the little boy   not more wiping up to do.

3. *Punctuate the following conversations.*

A young man was hoping to visit a drive-in theatre and he rang
the weather bureau.

a Hello is that the weather bureau   he asked
Yes it certainly is   replied the weather announcer
Well what are the chances of a shower tonight   the youth
asked
Its all right with me   Take one if you like   replied the weather
announcer

b were you able to see him   asked jack
no   replied steve   i had no luck at all
well you   ll have to try tomorrow   explained jack
yes i suppose so   sighed steve   but it really is annoying

Punctuation

 Apostrophes
Apostrophes are used in contractions to show that letters have been left out. Apostrophes are also used to show possession.

Contractions

wouldn't	would not
can't	cannot
we'll	we will
doesn't	does not
it's	it is or it has
I'd	I had
I'm	I am

Possession

An apostrophe is used to show ownership. It goes after the owner's name and before the s.

The boy's book is over there.
The girl's computer doesn't work.
The horse's mane was wet.
The men's toilet is over there.

Plurals

*If there is more than one owner and the word ends in **s** the apostrophe still goes after the name but no **s** is added.*
The boys' team is playing the girls' team tomorrow.

REMEMBER
You don't use apostrophes in these personal pronouns —
its hers his ours yours

Its and it's
Its claws were very long.	personal pronoun
It's over there.	Shortened form of 'It is over there'.
It's been a long time.	Shortened form of 'It has been a long time'.

1. *Where would the apostrophes be placed in these sentences?*

a His uncles car was beside my neighbours house.
b The monkeys antics were the zoos main attraction.
c Many cars headlights shone brightly on the mans statue.
d The fishermans haul was brought in on my friends boat.
e Womens jobs are as important as mens jobs.

2. *Rewrite the following and finish each sentence.*
The first one has been done for you.

a The crops of the farmers

The farmers' crops were ruined.

b The dress of the girl

_____

c The marbles of the boys

_____

d The coats of the ladies

_____

e The gowns of the princesses

_____

f The slippers of my father

_____

g The horse of my neighbour

_____

h The coat of the lady

_____

i The car of my uncle

_____

Punctuation

Direct speech is when we write down the exact speech that a speaker uses.
Indirect speech reports what was said.

Direct speech
"I have completed the work", said Ralph.
"It was a wonderful show", explained Emily.
"Can you move your car?", asked Geoff.

Indirect speech reports what was said, not using the exact words.
Ralph said that he had finished the work.
Emily explained that it was a wonderful show.
Geoff asked you to move the car.

Dashes — and hyphens -
The dash is used to show a distinct break in a sentence.
The ship was thrown onto the rocks, broke up and sank within a few minutes — not one survivor was found.

Hyphens are used in some compound words.
non-English speaking   mother-in-law
five-eighths   full-time work

I. *Are these sentences direct or indirect speech?*

a The man replied that he had been to the dentist.

_____

b "Where did you put my axe?" asked the woodcutter.

_____

c The woman complained that the boat was very uncomfortable.

_____

2. *Change the following to indirect speech.*

a "I have done that many times", said Alan.

_____

b The announcer said, "The game is under way".

_____

The girl cried, "I think I've lost it".

_____

3. *Change from indirect to direct speech.*

a The proud athlete claimed that he had never been beaten in a 5000 metre race.

_____

b The woman next to Tim stated that the shop was the best in town.

_____

c Without delay, Alan replied that he would finish the work.

_____

4. *Add punctuation to the following sentences.*

a who walked on the wet paint   asked the workman angrily
b how was the window broken   asked the woman in the green house
c where   enquired the tall stranger   could I purchase a roll of film

Te
ty

Text Types

A text is any meaningful written or spoken message. It is **communication**. In writing or speaking we can create texts and by reading or listening we can interpret texts.

Texts can be divided into different types.

TEXT TYPES

Literary texts
Narrative
- moral tales
- myths
- realistic stories
- fantasy
- science fiction
- Aboriginal dreaming stories

Drama
- plays
- film scripts
- radio plays

Poetry
- lyrics
- limericks
- sonnets
- verse

Factual texts
Discussion
- debates
- talk-back radio
- conversation

Explanation
- textbooks
- scientific writing
- spoken presentations

Exposition
- advertisements
- lectures

Information Report
- documentaries
- announcements
- reference books

Procedure
- instructions
- directions
- recipes

Recount
- diaries
- newspaper articles

As you study different texts add them to this table.
Classify them according to text type.

LITERARY TEXTS	FACTUAL TEXTS
Narrative	Information Report
	Procedure
Drama	Exposition
	Discussion
	Recount
Poetry	Explanation

Narrative text

Narrative texts <u>tell a story</u>. They entertain and instruct the reader, listener or viewer.

Basic structure

Orientation   — who or what is involved.
where and when is the story set.

Complication   — usual life of characters is interrupted, which adds tension and makes the story interesting.

Series of events — events that occur because of the complication.

Resolution — things are resolved.

Comment or coda — moral or comment from main character or narrator may be implicit or explicit.

Distinctive grammar

Use of nouns — particular person, place or thing.
Detailed descriptions of characters and setting.
Use of adverbs (how, when, where, why) to describe place and time.
Action verbs to describe the events.
Verbs for feeling, thinking or saying.
Connecting words to sequence events in time such as then, afterwards, since, before.

Examples
Realistic stories, tales, fables, science fiction, fantasy, myths,

The Enemies

Jake and Elijah were enemies on a voyage in the same small boat. Naturally each tried to place himself as far as possible from the other. Elijah stayed in the front, or bow, of the boat while Jake remained in the back, or stern. Without warning, a great storm arose and the boat began to sink.

"Which end of the boat will sink first?" asked Jake.

"The bow will go down first," replied the captain.

"That's fine," said Jake. "Then I can have the satisfaction of watching Elijah, my enemy, drown."

But of course Jake's revenge was short, for his end of the boat sank soon afterward, and he too was drowned. So, do not rejoice in another's misfortune when you are both in the same boat.

(from Aesop)

ORIENTATION — Two enemies, Jake and Elijah in a boat .
COMPLICATION — The boat starts to sink.
EVENTS — Jake questions the captain and comments.
RESOLUTION — The boat sinks and they are both drowned.
CODA — The moral of the story – do not rejoice in another's misfortune when you are both in the same boat.

Alice, the Copy Dog

One day Mum brought home a big, black dog and asked me to look after it. It belonged to Mr Jakes who works at her office. Mr Jakes was in hospital for a few days. Mum said the dog's name was Alice. Funny name for such an ugly dog, I thought. Mum knew I hated dogs. How could she promise Mr Jakes that I'd look after it?

I stomped down the back stairs and took Alice down to the park to play ball. After one throw the ball was covered in slobbery drool. Disgusting! I threw the wet, sticky ball again and it landed in the long grass. Alice looked at me curiously and sat down. 'Well go and get it,' I said. She just sat there.

What a lazy dog! I started to go and get it myself but each time I took a step, Alice took a step and each time I stopped, Alice stopped. I started to run and Alice ran too. I turned and ran the other way. Alice followed. I ran zig zags. Alice ran zig zags. I jumped in the air. Alice jumped in the air. 'You're a crazy copy dog!' I called out.

Then I fell down in a heap and rolled on my back, panting. Alice rolled on her back too. Then she pounced on me and slobbered all over my face. It was pretty revolting—but I started to laugh and I couldn't stop. Alice looked very pleased with herself. I guess dogs aren't so bad after all.

STUDENT ANALYSIS

1. *What is the orientation in 'Alice, the Copy Dog'?*

_____

_____

2. *What is the complication?*

_____

_____

3. *In point form, list the series of events that follow the complication.*

_____

_____

4. *What is the resolution?*

_____

5. *What is the coda?*

_____

6. *List the nouns that represent people, places or things in the story.*

_____

7. *List the verbs used in the story. Classify them according to their function in the story as doing or **acting** verbs, **thinking** or feeling verbs, **saying** or **asking** verbs, or **being** verbs.*

doing or acting verbs	thinking or feeling verbs	saying or asking verbs	being verbs
brought	knew	said	belonged

Discussion text

Discussions give <u>differing views</u> on an issue.

Basic structure
• *Opening statement of the issue.*
• *The different points of view.*
• *Concluding recommendation.*

Distinctive grammar

Common nouns — the environment, politicians, school children.
Being verbs for the line of argument ie. is, was, are.
Thinking and feeling verbs — I feel, I'd like.

Explanation text

Explanations tell <u>how or why</u> something happens.

Basic structure
• *Introduce the topic to be explained.*
• *Step by step series of statements.*
• *Conclusion – brief overview.*

School tuck shops

Many students, teachers and parents have strong views about the type of food sold in the school tuck shop.

Many students believe that they should have the right to choose what they would like to eat and how they spend their money. They would like the school tuck shop to sell a wider variety of food, including fast food and lollies.

However, some parents disagree. They believe that the school should encourage students to develop healthy eating habits. These parents believe the school tuck shop should sell only healthy food.

On the other hand, some parents and teachers are worried that if the tuck shop does not sell the type of food the students want to buy, then it will lose profits. These parents and teachers see these profits as a vital part of fundraising to buy badly needed resources for the school.

In summary, there is enough concern to warrant further investigation into the tuck shop and its policies.

A discussion about weekends

Chris   What are you doing this weekend?

Emma   Well, first thing Saturday I'm playing tennis, and then we're all going shopping. Then we'll probably go to the beach after lunch. On Sunday we're going to Leura to visit Nan. What about you?

Chris   Nothing. Just playing around the house.

Emma   That sounds great. I'm sick of going out all the time. We're never at home, with sports and picnics and visiting people. I'd love to have a quiet weekend at home.

Chris   I'll swap any day. Hanging around the house all the time is boring.

Emma   You're like my mum. She likes to keep busy too.

STUDENT ANALYSIS

1. What is the discussion about?

2. What are the two views on this issue?

3. Which common nouns are used?

4. List all the thinking and feeling verbs used in the discussion.

5. Write all the contractions in their expanded form.

Procedure text

Procedural texts give instructions or descriptions of <u>how to do something</u>.

Basic structure

• *The aim of the instructions.*
• *Materials required (optional).*
• *Series of steps in logical order (often numbered).*

Distinctive grammar

Common nouns.
Action verbs.
Imperative mood — commands.
Chronological order.
Timeless present tense.

Examples

Directions, instuctions, recipes.

EXAMPLE

How to plant an Ironbark Tree
(Eucalyptus sieberiana)

Things you need: Spade, water, ironbark potplant.

1. Choose a spot that gets plenty of sun.
2. Dig a hole twice the size of the pot.
3. Fill the hole with water and wait till the water has drained away.
4. Hold the stem of the tree and tap the pot to free it.
5. Tease the roots loose.
6. Place the tree in the hole so that the base of the stem is level with the soil.
7. Fill the hole with soil.
8. Firmly press the soil around the plant.
9. Water well.
10. Keep the soil around your *Eucalyptus sieberiana* moist for at least a week.

Enjoy watching your tree grow!!

ACTIVITY

Try writing a procedure for your favourite game or sport.

Exposition text

Exposition texts persuade an audience to adopt a <u>certain</u> opinion or to buy a <u>particular</u> product.

Basic structure
- *Outline the position held.*
- *Stages in argument.*
- *Summing up.*

Distinctive grammar

Common and collective nouns.
High degree of certainty.
Connecting words that show cause.
Timeless present tense.
Emotive language.

Examples

Advertisements, speeches, editorials, political texts.

STUDENT ANALYSIS

At last! A toothpaste that puts the slime into smile!
It's sticky!
It's sweet!
You'll love it!
We've use the latest scientific ingredients
FLOURIOXIDATE and DENTOCHLORISTAT
to guarantee you a real flouro smile!
Don't be the last to try it!

1. Who would this advertisement appeal to?

_____

2. List the adjectives used to make the product sound good.

_____

3. Why has the writer of the advertisement used technical terminology?

_____

4. What emotive language does the advertisement contain?

_____

5. Why has this emotive language been used?

_____

6. What doesn't the advertisement tell you about the new toothpaste?

_____

_____

7. Write an advertisement for another everyday product.

Report text

An information report gives a factual description of a thing or animal

Basic structure

• *Introduction — often a definition.*
• *Sequenced facts.*
• *Rounding off statement (optional).*

Distinctive grammar

Common nouns to describe classes of things.
Technical terms.
The topic name is repeated often.
Use of paragraphs to organise the facts.
The first sentence in each paragraph introduces a new aspect of the topic.
Timeless present tense.
Being and having verbs describe relationships between aspects of the topic.
Action verbs describe behaviour.

Examples

Scientific texts, lectures, text books, reference books.

Ants

Ants are six-legged insects. There are many varieties of ants differing in size, colour and habitat—but they all have some physical and social features in common.

Ants have segmented bodies with hard exoskeletons. Each has a head, abdomen and thorax with six legs, two eyes, two feelers, and pincer-like jaws.

Ants live together in large nests. Their behaviour serves the colony rather than the individual. One ant, the queen, lays all the eggs for the whole nest. She is attended by worker ants which can carry up to eight times their own weight.

Ants find their way by light patterns, by special sense organs in the joints of their legs and by chemical trails which they leave between the nest and food sources.

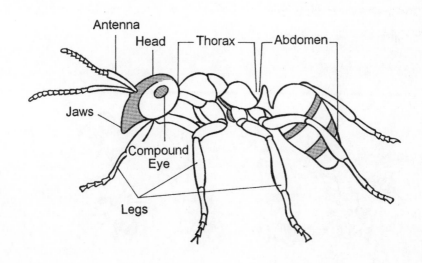

Bees

Honeybees are flying insects that make honey to feed their young.

Like all insects, bees have six legs, three body sections and two antennae. They also have a pair of wings and can fly many kilometres every day.

Bees live in colonies called hives. A bee hive may have as many as 50 000 bees. The hive is built out of beeswax and has different compartments for the queen, the eggs, the developing bees and the honeycomb.

There is one queen bee in each hive. Her job is to lay all the eggs. Male bees are called drones. Their only job is to mate with the queen.

Female bees are called workers. They guard the hive, build the honeycomb, clean the empty cells, take care of the young bees and collect nectar, pollen and water. They might visit up to five hundred flowers in a day to collect pollen and nectar. It takes one thousand bee trips to make just one teaspoon of honey!

Bees communicate by performing a dance. The dance tells the other bees the direction of the flowers, for example if the bees dance in circles it means the flowers are close to the hive.

This insect really is as busy as a bee!

STUDENT ANALYSIS

1. Write a list of the **action** verbs that appear in the text.

_____

_____

_____

2. List the **being** or **having** verbs that appear in the text.

_____

_____

3. The report is organised in paragraphs. What new aspect of the topic is introduced in:

paragraph 2? _____

paragraph 3? _____

paragraph 4? _____

paragraph 5? _____

paragraph 6? _____

4. Draw a diagram to represent some of the information in the report.

Recount text

Recount texts retell events in the order in which they occurred.

Basic structure
• *Orientation — introduces who, where and when.*
• *Events retold in chronological order.*
• *Personal comment (usually).*

Distinctive grammar

Past tense action verbs.
Thinking and feeling verbs to express personal concern.
Use of adverbs (how, when, where, why) to describe place and time.
Connecting words to link events through time — and then, afterwards, later.

Examples

News items, current affairs programs, documentaries, letters, conversations.

BUSHFIRE

8 people injured

EIGHT PEOPLE WERE INJURED AS A BUSHFIRE SWEPT THROUGH THE LOWER BLUE MOUNTAINS, WEST OF SYDNEY, YESTERDAY.

The fire started near the town of Lawson. It rapidly took hold as gale force winds swept through the area. Firefighters from the surrounding areas, plus many volunteers, rushed to the scene.

The bushfire raged through the night before firefighters gained control early this morning. All the injured, including one firefighter, were taken to Westmead Hospital where they are reported to be in a stable condition. Firefighters are still mopping up and the damage is being assessed.

Geoff the biker

Early last Sunday a man drove up our driveway on a noisy, black motorcycle. He had on black leather pants, a black leather jacket and a helmet. I'd never seen him before.

As I was watching him park the bike and take off his helmet, my father came running out the front door. He ran down towards the man and the motorcycle. At first I couldn't tell whether he was angry or glad. Then the man in black leather and my Dad gave each other a big hug.

They spent the next ten minutes laughing and talking before coming into the house. My father said, "This is Geoff, Geoff and I went to school together". Geoff shook my hand.

After a while, Geoff showed me his bike, it was a Ducati. Dad said I could go for a ride with Geoff. I couldn't believe it, I'd never been on a motorbike before.

I can hardly describe how it felt, but it was great. It was like flying and I can't wait to do it again.

STUDENT ANALYSIS

I. *In chronological order, list the events that the author recounts.*

_____

_____

_____

_____

_____

_____

2. *List all the past tense verbs that appear in the recount.*

_____

_____

3. *Why is this tense used?*

_____

_____

4. *How do you feel about the author? What aspects of the text make you feel this way?*

_____

_____

_____

Explanation text

Explanation texts tell **how or why** something happens.

Basic structure

- *Introduce the topic to be explained.*
- *Series of statements.*
- *Conclusion.*

Distinctive grammar

Action verbs — turns, heats, pulls.
Connecting words to link events in time order or to show a cause and effect relationship — next, after that, this causes.
Technical terms.
Passive voice.

Examples

Scientific or historical topics.

Why is my skin wrinkled when I get out of the bath?

As you soak in the warm bath water your skin gets hot. The heat causes the blood to flow into the tips of your fingers and toes. This blood makes your fingers and toes look puffy. At the same time, the soapy water strips the natural oils off your skin. When you get out of the bath, your fingers and toes cool off. As they cool, the blood moves further back again. This makes the puffiness disappear and your skin (without its oil) looks wrinkled.

How the TV Remote Control Works

When a button is pressed on the remote control, the battery inside sends out electricity. The electricity travels to a light-emitting diode (LED). The LED then sends out a beam of infrared light. This beam carries a signal which tells which button was pushed on the remote control. When the beam reaches the receiver in the television, the receiver decodes the signal. Hey presto! The television switches channels!

ACTIVITY PAGE

STUDENT ANALYSIS

1. What is the introduction to the explanation?

_____

_____

2. What is the conclusion?.

_____

_____

3. List the action verbs used in the explanation.

_____

_____

_____

4. List the words used in the explanation to link the events in time order.

_____

_____

5. Draw a flow chart to represent the explanation.

Answers

UNIT 1
1. Mum, Dad, Clare, Hugh, Campbelltown, suburb, Sydney, breeder, border collie pups, excitement, city, buildings, blocks, trees, farm
2. sons, babies, mice, wolves, halves, knives, feet, loaves
4. Jay, Simba, February, Zimbabwe
5. herd, team, army
6. elephant, bottle glue, dog, cloud, pencil
7. lions — pride, flowers — bunch, soldiers — army, fish — school, wood — stack, sheep — mob

UNIT 2
1. crates of animals, the skiff with the torn sail, Many of the books which I owned, some very rich desserts, The bird in the huge nest
5. a The large, hairy dog with big teeth leapt at me.
   b There's a huge, green, slobbering monster running after me.

UNIT 3
1. a He, his b you, yourself, their c I, your, I, them, you d who, she
2. a James opened his book and got his pencil and started his home-work.
   b We saw the boys when their sister told us where they were playing.
3. her, She, her, It, them, her, she, her, They, her, you
4. a They hurt themselves.
   b They have their books with them.
   c They helped themselves.

UNIT 4
1. a I, our b I c who d which e I f who
2. a I b I c which d who e I me g who h which
3. a Don't leave the room unless I tell you.
   b 'Why were you here?' she asked.

UNIT 5
1. a past b in c on d near
2. a T b F c T d F e T f F g H h T i F
3. a On the trip, over the desert, through difficult terrain
   b over the hill, to the blue lake, near the homestead
   c down the road, on her bike

UNIT 6
1.

past	present	future
rang	is ringing	will ring
left	is leaving	will leave
brought	is bringing	will bring
fenced	is fencing	will fence
dropped	is dropping	will drop
told	is telling	will tell

2. a seen b seeing c seen d saw
3. a done b did c doing d Does
4. a will see b will play c will go
5. a having-being b thinking c action

UNIT 7
2. a will be b has been c been d is
5. a finished, active b was driven, passive c played, active
6. a The hole in the fence was discovered by Christina.
   b The art student completed the painting.

UNIT 8
1. a mending b running c fishing d crying e buying
3. a She dives into the pool.
   b They drive past us.
   c I tell him.
   d Josh travels by bus to the game.
   e The police follow the car.
4. a ride b mean c choose d deal e understand f meet

UNIT 9 1 a has been regularly making
b have been grazing
c had been known to tell
d wanted to complete
e have been delivering
f is finished
2 a having-being b thinking
c action d saying
3 started to feel; to do; could finish;
decided to keep working; began
to growl

UNIT 11 1 comparative   superlative
smaller   smallest
lovelier   lovliest
better   best
more interesting most interesting
cleaner   cleanest
more difficult   most difficult
unhappier   unhappiest
simpler or more simplest or most
simple   simple
2 a taller b tallest c taller d tallest
3 a more splendid b most splendid
5 a more b most c more d most

UNIT 12 2 tired, running, excited, bored,
interesting, scared, thrilled

UNIT 13 1 a delightfully b soon c greedily
d there e eagerly f sometimes
3 a neatly b strangely c noisily
5 a It rained heavily this afternoon.
b It is a particularly heavy box.
c This is the first really good book
I've bought.

UNIT 14 3 a (i) b (ii) c (i) d (i) e (ii)
f (i) g (i)

UNIT 15 1 a question b command
c statement d exclamation
e question f request
2 a no b no c yes d no e yes
f no g yes
3 a found b went c go d gave
e told f collected

UNIT 16 1 b, c, d
2 a Here are the cattle that ate
the crops.
b Romana owns the car that is
by the garage.
3 a The students came here.
They did not complete the work.
b I enjoyed the show. It was full
of action.
4 a no b no c no d yes
5 a Dario went to the field and
he climbed the mountain.
b Sally plays the piano but she
cannot play the flute.
c My brother goes to the class
and he may go to the movies.

UNIT 18 1 a Where b What c Who d How
e What f Who g How

UNIT 19 1 a is b was delivered c do
2 a she b They c the lights
3 a the letter b this c the chairs
4 a her b Linda c me
5 b subject verb object
c subject verb object
d object subject verb
6 a are collecting b were grazing
c are waiting d were held up

UNIT 20 1 a All of the children b I c Care
and attention to detail d A box
2 a to the beach on the weekend
b very noisy c with a green lid
d with old toys
3 a circumstance, participants,
process, participants, circumstance
b participants, process, participants,
c participants, process,
circumstance
d circumstance, participant,
process, participants

UNIT 21 1 a a, an, a b a, a, an c a d a, a e an
2 a, a, The, a, an, the, the
3 a a, The b an, the c a, the d a, The

UNIT 22 1 a but b nor c and d and e or
3 a There are the parrots and the galahs.
b Fotini owns the car but it isn't working.
c The boys went into town and saw a movie.
4 a for b if, yet c and d before or until
5 but, and, for, and, so, until, because

UNIT 23 1 a I don't know anything.
b No one cares about me.
c I never go anywhere.
2 a I just saw him downstairs.
3 a I already did it.
b The girls have done it already.
4 a I was going to go but it cost too much.
b There are too many feral cats.
c The girls were pushed to and fro.
5 a That box should have been picked up hours ago.
b I should have known he would be late.

UNIT 25 1 a Jack, I, Jungle Patrol, July
b I, Hard Labour, Norfolk Island
c On, Wednesday, Phil, Romana, Bathurst, Ellendale Stud
d Mrs J C Curry, Coffs Harbour Public School
e In, February, I, Anson Island
f In, Australian Outback, Alice Springs
2 a TFE b L c cm d Mrs e St
f QANTAS g ACT h Wed i CD
j VCR k Capt. l NT m Dr
3 impossible. distance. running. burned. couldn't. him.

UNIT 26 1 a Help! They are getting away.
b "Why are you here?" asked Tom.
c "Quick, get out of here!" shouted Joan.
d "What is the capital of Tasmania?" enquired Tom.
e "What a great save!" said the reporter excitedly.
f "How do you reach Lake Placid?" asked Lee.
g I asked him what he saw.
h "What a surprise! Who organised this?" asked Mum.
3 a There were many birds in the cage: finches, sparrows, lovebirds, pigeons and galahs.
b Carrie had driven several cars: a Ferrari, a Porsche, a BMW, an Audi and a Bentley.
c There were books on many subjects in the pile: maths, English, social studies and computers.

UNIT 27 1 a Many of the young, frisky ponies galloped across the paddock.
b Pelicans, ducks and swans were on the lake.
c The cold, damp room was very gloomy.
d Nancy, Annie, Loma and May went to Cairns.
d A wise, old, brown owl was sitting in the tree.
f Strange, ghostly, mysterious shapes were seen.
g Speedboats, cruisers, kayaks and yachts were out on the river.
h Ponies, quarter-horses, appaloosas and Australian stock horses were at the show.
i Of course, the rider came to no harm.
j Last year, the students played football on the newly built oval and enjoyed swimming in the new Olympic pool. k My big brother, Mat, lives in Singapore.
l "Excuse me, can you tell me where the shopping centre is?"
m Did you know that Miss Jenkins, the Year 4 teacher, is away today?
2 a I'm afraid of the dark.
b I don't like bugs, mice and rats.
c The duck was small, wet, cold and sad.

d There I was, alone, scared and hungry.
e She saw a beautiful, craggy, old tree.
f Mr Hines, the principal, said we could go.

UNIT 28 l a "He is going to the show", said Rhonda.
b "Mark saw the young filly!" cried Bill.
c "Take it out at once", said Dad.
d "I'm sure I know the answer," replied Andrew.
e "Look out for the falling brick!" shouted Amanda.
2 a "The girl", he replied, "can hardly lift it."
b "Well", the stranger asked, "where is the gift?"
c "If you travel south", he explained, "you will reach the forest."
d "This view", announced the driver, "is the most famous in the district."
e "Oh, dear", groaned the little boy, "not more wiping up to do."
3 a "Hullo, is that the weather bureau?" he asked.
"Yes, it certainly is", replied the weather recorder.
"Well, what are the chances of a shower tonight?" the youth asked.
"It's all right with me. Take one if you like", replied the weather recorder.
b "Were you able to see him?" asked Jack.
"No", replied Steve, "I had no luck at all".
"Well, you'll have to try tomorrow", explained Jack.
"Yes, I suppose so", sighed Steve, "but it really is annoying".

UNIT 29 l a uncle's, neighbor's b monkey's, zoo's c cars', man's d fisherman's, friend's e women's, men's
2 b The girl's dress c The boys' marbles d The ladies' coats e The princesses' gowns f My father's slippers g My neighbour's horse h The lady's coat i My uncle's car

UNIT 30 l a indirect b direct c indirect
2 a Alan said that he has done that many times.
b The announcer said that the game is just about to get under way.
c The girl cried that she has lost it.
3 a "I have never been beaten in a 5000 metre race", claimed the proud athlete.
b "This shop is the best in town", stated the woman next to him.
c "Without delay", Alan replied, "I will finish the work."
4 a "Who walked on the wet paint?" asked the workman, angrily.
b "How was the window broken?" asked the woman in the green house.
c "Where", enquired the tall stranger, "could I purchase a roll of film?"

Glossary

abstract nouns: names of feelings and ideas. p10

action verbs: the doing verbs — run, jump, climb. p22, 24, 28

active voice: the active voice is used to show that the subject of sentence is the doer of the action. p24

Steve carried the box.

(carried is a verb in the active voice).

adjective: describing words telling what kind, how many, how much, which person or thing. p32

adjective clause: a group of words in a complex sentence with a finite verb, doing the work of an adjective. (describing telling about).

I saw the car which had a red roof.

(which had a red roof is an adjective clause).

adjective phrase: a group of words without a finite verb, doing the work of an adjective (describing or telling about).

The box with the red lid is new.

(with the red lid is an adjective phrase).

adverb: a word which modifies or tells about verbs adjectives or other adverbs. p38, 40

He will go soon.

(soon is an adverb telling about when).

adverb clause: a group of words in a complex sentence with a finite verb doing the work of an adverb (modifying or telling about).

He worked as if he was tired.

(as if he was tired is an adverb clause).

adverb phrase: a group of words without a finite verb doing the work of an adverb (modifying or telling about).

He worked as if he was tired.

(as if he was tired is an adverb clause).

article: 'the' is the definite article. it refers to a particular person, place, animal or thing. 'A' and `an' are the indefinite articles. p58

attribute: an adjective which describes a noun. They include classifiers, describers, numeratives and determiners. p32

auxiliary verb: part of a main verb, a helping verb.
He has been taking the medicine. p24
(has been are auxiliary verbs).

being verb: verbs that are relational processes — is, was. p22, 24

case: the relationship between a noun or pronouns and other parts of speech is called case. There are three cases — nominative, objective, possessive. p76

circumstance: is an adverb, prepositional phrase or noun group that tells how, when, where or why an action is taking place. p54

classifiers: adjectives that group or classify nouns — gum trees, spelling books.

clause: a group of words with a finite verb and a subject. It can be a simple sentence. e.g. I walked to school, or it can be part of a complex or compound sentence. p46

I saw the car which had a red roof.

(contains two clauses).

closed questions questions which require a simple yes/no answer.

cohesion: is the linking of ideas in a piece of writing. p14,60

collective nouns: names for collections of people or things — team, navy. p10

command: a clause or simple sentence — a request, directive or in some cases providing a warning or invitation.

common gender: is used when the noun or pronoun could be either masculine or feminine gender.

The children took their coats.

(children and their are both common gender).

common nouns: names of common objects. p10

(spider, shovel, cloud, tree are common nouns).

comparative degree: used to describe the form of adjective or adverb used when comparing two things. p34, 40

She is taller than Laura.

(taller is comparative).

He walked slower than his brother.

(slower is comparative).

complement: usually appears after a finite verb in a situation where the subject is actually the same 'thing' as the complement.

The box is a light one.

(box is the subject, one is the complement).

complex sentence: made up of a principal clause and one or more subordinate clauses, either adverb, adjective or noun clauses. p46

compound sentence: made up of two or more clauses both of which are principal clauses. p46

compound verbs: verbs with one or more auxiliary verbs. p24

conjunction: is a joining word that joins words, phrases and clauses. p60

connecting words: words that join words, phrases and clauses to make more complex sentences. Also known as conjunctions. p60

declarative mode: the mood used in statements. p48

degrees of comparison: term used to describe the use of adjectives and adverbs that compare.
Laura is tall.(positive degree) Laura is taller than Amanda.(comparative degree) Laura is the tallest in her class.(superlative degree). p34,40

demonstrative pronouns: refer to the noun they stand for — those, these, that, this.

dependent clause: a clause that cannot stand on its own. Needs an independent clause to make a complete sentence. p46

describer: an adjective that describes a noun or pronoun. p32

It was a stunted bush.

(stunted is a descriptive adjective).

determiner: an adjective that points out which noun or pronoun. p32

That car is brand new.

(that is a determiner adjective).

embedded clause: is a clause which is placed between the noun it tells about and the rest of the sentence. p46

The car that has a sunroof is mine.

(that has a sunroof is an embedded clause).

embedded phrase: is a phrase which is placed between the noun it tells about and the rest of the sentence. p46

The car with a sunroof is brand new.

(with a sunroof is an embedded phrase).

exclamation: abrupt or excited sentence ending with a !. p44

feminine gender: is used when the noun or pronoun is female

Hayley took her book.

(Hayley and her are feminine gender).

field: is the subject matter, or content of a piece of writing. p64

finite verb: a verb or verb group which has a subject. p22

first person: is the form of pronoun used by the person speaking. — I, we.

future tense : a verb in the future tense is one where the action will take place in the future. p22

He will go the movies.
(will go is future tense).

gender: nouns and pronouns have gender. They can be masculine gender (male), feminine gender (female), common gender (either male nor female) or neuter gender, (neither male nor female).

gerund: a verb used as a noun by adding ~'ing' to the stem. His swimming is excellent.

(swimming is a gerund).

having verb: verbs that are relational processes — has, have. p22, 24, 28

head word: Is the main word in a word group.

several young children
has been taking
(children and taking are head words).

imperative mood: the mood used in commands. p48

Carry this bottle,
(command — imperative mood).

indefinite pronouns: do not refer to any particular person, place or thing — no—one, nothing.

independent clause: a clause that can stand on its own. A simple sentence is an independent clause. p46

infinite verbs: verbs that do not have a subject are termed infinite verbs. Infinitives, and participles are infinite verbs.

infinitive: the infinitive is the name of the verb — usually begins with the word to. p26

To catch him was difficult.
(to catch is an infinitive).

interjection: is used to express surprise or sudden emotion and is usuallly followed by an exclamation mark.

Oh! I've broken it.
(Oh! is an interjection).

interrogative mood: the mood used in questions. p48

interrogative pronouns: are used in questions — who, what.

intransitive verbs: a verb which does not have an object is called intransitive.

He went to the party.
(the verb went does not have an object — it is intransitive).

irregular verbs: verbs where the past tense and the past participle are not formed in the usual way are called irregular verbs. p26

talk, talked, have talked (regular).
speak, spoke, have spoken (irregular).

manner adverbs: tell how the action was done. p40

masculine gender: is used when the noun or pronoun is male.

Steve took his back.
(Steve and his are masculine gender).

modality: how language is used to express the difference between possibility and certainty. p48

mode: the means of communication — written, spoken etc.

modifier: an adverb or an adverb group.

mood: sentences can be either indicative, imperative or subjunctive mood. Mood is shown by the way the subject and the finite verb are placed. p48

Statements are indicative mood.

Commands are imperative mood.

Sentences expressing doubt are subjunctive mood.

narrative: texts that tell a story.

neuter gender: is used when the noun or pronoun is neither masculine nor feminine

The block is on the table.
(block is neuter gender).

non-finite/verb: an infinite verb, one that does not have a subject.

nominalisation: the building of nouns or noun groups from verbs. p96

He collected the posters the same day (verb).

His collection of the posters was done the same day (noun).

nominative case: words that are the subject of a finite verb are nominative case.

noun: a naming word. The name of a person, place, thing or feeling. p10

noun clause: a group of words with a finite verb that does the work of a noun in a sentence. p12

What he has done is a terrible mistake.
(what he has done is a noun clause).

noun groups: a group of words with a noun as head word and other words, nouns, adjectives, articles included — makes up a participant.

number: nouns or pronouns can be singular number. (talking about one thing) or plural number (talking about more than one thing). p10

The car is behind the garages.

(car is singular, garages is plural).

numerative: an adjective that indicates the number of things. p32

Few people were there.
(Few is a numerative adjective).

object (direct): the direct object is the receiver of the action. It is found by asking the question —
What did (subject) (verb)? p52

Tom ate the cake.

(cake is the direct object).

object (indirect): the indirect object is the person or thing to whom the object is supplied. p52

He gave the money to her.
(money is the direct object).

(her is the indirect object).

objective case: words that are the objects of verbs and prepositions are said to be in the objective case.
Jill likes ice-cream. (ice-cream is in the objective case)

open questions: require a long response. p50

open word classes: groups of words that can be added to as new ideas and inventions are introduced into society — nouns, verbs, adjectives and adverbs.

opinion: a personal view.

participants: the noun groups, adjective groups and adjective phrases that are involved in the processes in sentences. p12, 54.

participle: an infinite verb — often used with auxiliary verbs. p26

(He has broken the glass — participle).

passive voice: the passive voice focuses on the person or thing affected by the action. p24

past tense: a verb in the past tense is one where the action takes place in the past. p22

He went to the show.
(went is past tense).

person: is the term used to describe the form of pronoun used.

first person — person speaking I, we.
second person — person spoken to you, your.
third person — person spoke about he, them.

personal pronouns: are used instead of persons — she, you, he, they. p14

phrases: a group of words without a finite verb. p18

place adverbs: tell where the action happened. p40

plural number: nouns or pronouns can be plural number. Plural means more than one thing — cars, their, garages. p10

positive degree: the form of adjective or adverb used to describe a single thing. She is a tall girl. p40

possessive case: words that own other things are said to be in the possessive case.
This is Mary's book. This is her book.
(Mary's and her are possessive case).

possessive pronouns: show ownership — yours, mine. p14

predicate: a simple sentence consists of a subject and predicate. The predicate contains a finite verb.

prepositions: relate one thing to another and are always followed by a noun or a pronoun. They often refer to the position of things.
He went to the shop. (to is the preposition). p18

prepositional phrase: a group of words without a verb that starts with a preposition. p18

present tense: a verb where the action is taking place now. p22

principal clause: makes sense on its own — an independent clause. p46

process: verbs or verb groups in sentences — the activities — action, thinking, saying, having and being words. p28, 54

pronoun: is a word that can be used instead of a noun. p14
She will go by herself to his place.
(she, herself, his are pronouns).

proper noun: the names of particular persons, places, things. p10
Sue went to Queensland last Christmas.
(Sue, Queensland, Christmas are proper nouns)

qualify: means to tell about. It is used to describe the action an adjective does.
Several animals were here.
(several is a qualifying adjective).

questions: a sentence that seeks an answer. These sentences always end with a question mark. p44, 48, 50

regular verb: verb where the past tense and the past participle are formed in the usual way adding ed, d, or t. p26
talk, talked, have talked (regular).
speak, spoke, have spoken (irregular).

relative pronoun: they are — who, whom, whose, which, that. p16

request: a type of command stated politely. p44, 48

rheme: the rest of the clause or sentence following the theme.

My brother has followed the car (rheme).

saying verb: verbs describing speaking — said, yelled, shouted. p22, 24, 28

second person: the term used to describe the form of pronoun when someone is spoken to. You take your gear away. (you and your are second person).

simple sentence: a sentence with one clause. p44

singular number: nouns or pronouns can be singular number. Singular number talks about one thing — boy, bike. p10

statement: a sentence where something is stated.
The boy ate the cake.(statement). p44, 48

subject: The subject of a sentence is the person or thing doing the action. Laura danced in the hall. (Laura is the subject). p52

subordinate clause: adds meaning to the independent clause. Also known as a dependent clause. p46

superlative degree: the form of adjective or adverb used when comparing more than two things. p34, 40

tense: verbs have tense (past, present, future, timeless present). Tense tells us whether the action is happening now, in the past, in the future or continues over time. p22

theme: the first part of a clause or sentence. It sets the scene for further information.
The workers completed the work.

thinking verb: verbs describing mental processes — believed, understood. p22, 24, 28

third person: the term used to describe the form of pronoun when speaking about someone or something.
They will be going to their house.
(they and their are third person).

time adverbs: tell when something happened. p40

timeless present: verbs that describe actions that continue over time.
Lions are good hunters.
(are is timeless present). p22

transitive verbs: a verb which has an object is transitive.
He collected the papers. (the verb collected has an object — papers).

verb: a word which tells of an action or state. It is a doing, saying, thinking, being or having word. p22-29

verb groups: a group of words that link closely to the main verb. Also known as processes. p28

verb to be: a verb that links a subject to a complement.
Jason is a doctor.
(is — verb to be, Jason — subject doctor — complement).

voice: verbs have what is called voice — active or passive. The two voices allow the same idea to be expressed in different ways.
Jim polished the floor — active.
The floor was polished by Jim — passive). p24

© 1996 P. Walker
ISBN 1864410604

Pascal Press
PO Box 250
Glebe 2037
(02) 5574844

Designed by Love Of Design Electronic Publishing.
Typesetting by Arc Typography.
Chapter title page illustrations by Majid Chekroun.
Printed by Australian Paper Group.

Index